One You One Me
Just the way God created us to be

Inspired by Angela Y. Nixon
Illustrated by Chandra Gunawan

JG| JENIS GROUP, LLC

One You, One Me Copyright © 2017

Any unauthorized reproduction, use, copying, distribution or sale of these materials – including words and illustrations – without written consent of the author is strictly prohibited. Federal law provides severe penalties for unauthorized reproduction, use, copying or distribution of copyrighted material.

_____

Book Cover design by Angela Y. Nixon
ISBN 978-1-942674-18-4
First Edition: November 2017

For bulk order prices or any other queries, please contact aynixon@jenisgroup.com

This book belongs to

_____

In the whole, wide world, across land and sea,
there is only one "you" and only one "me."
Have you not heard, you are one-of-a-kind!
A girl just like you, no one can find.
For each of us was made by God who is good.
He gave us something special, as only He could.

Can you raise your hands and say "thank you" to God?

Perhaps you are short, or maybe you are tall.
It really does not matter no, not at all!
Freckles dot my nose, but you don't have any.
Your hair has a lot of curls, but mine, not so many.
We can have fun together no matter how we look,
by playing ball, or swimming, or even reading a book.

What are your favorite ways to play?

Our skin might be dark, or medium or fair.
We might choose bright clothes,
or wear flowers in our hair.
No matter how we look, it should not keep us apart.
For God looks inside, deep into our hearts.
He wants us to love and care for each other
just as we care about our sisters and brothers.

What are ways you care for others?

Some kids wear braces to help fix their teeth.
Others need glasses to really help them see.
One girl likes to dance, while another likes to paint.
What do you like best? What fun things do you create?

You are great at something! What you like to do?

We like different foods,
and that is OK.
We can always eat
our lunch together anyway.
We will talk about what we want
to be when we are grown,
like a veterinarian, or the president
only God knows!
He has a plan for you
and for me one day.
If you asked Him about it, what do
you think He would say?

Go ahead, ask Him!

Sometimes it's easy to look at outer things,
like the way someone dresses
or the way someone sings.
But we should always be willing
to give a fair chance
we don't really know someone
after only one glance!
So use kind words, and always listen well.
Then you will make a friend
who has a wonderful story to tell.

Are you good at listening?

By spending time together, we can learn many things.
Like what our favorite colors are,
or if we like green beans.
We can have a picnic or play tag outside,
take a walk around the block or go on a bicycle ride.

I like picnics. Do you?

Another way to be the very best we can,
is to always be willing to lend a helping hand.
Climb a tree to rescue a kitty that is afraid.
Laugh at a funny joke that another friend made.
Stop to help a younger person, and teach them to tie their shoes.
These things make God smile,
and they make me smile too!

What makes you smile?

Most of all, we are loved by Jesus,
and made to love Him.
Do you know the Savior? Where should I begin?
"God so loved the world, that He gave His only Son,"
to die for all the wrong things
we have ever done.
And when we believe in the
precious name of Jesus,
He draws us to Himself nothing more
could ever please us.

Do you believe in Jesus?

————

So, never forget that you are one-of-a-kind.
No one "just like you" will anyone ever find.
For in the whole, wide world, across land and sea,
there is only one "you" and only one "me."

The End

About the Author

Angela Nixon aspires to do God's will for her life.
She is a wife and mother of four children.

Angela is a God-fearing
and God-loving woman who
loves people and she aspires to inspire
others through the gifts
and talents God has given her.

Do you have a desire to write and need direction?
Please contact Angela Y. Nixon
aynixon@jenisgroup.com

www.ingramcontent.com/pod-product-compliance
Lightning Source LLC
Chambersburg PA
CBHW050759110526
44588CB00002B/51